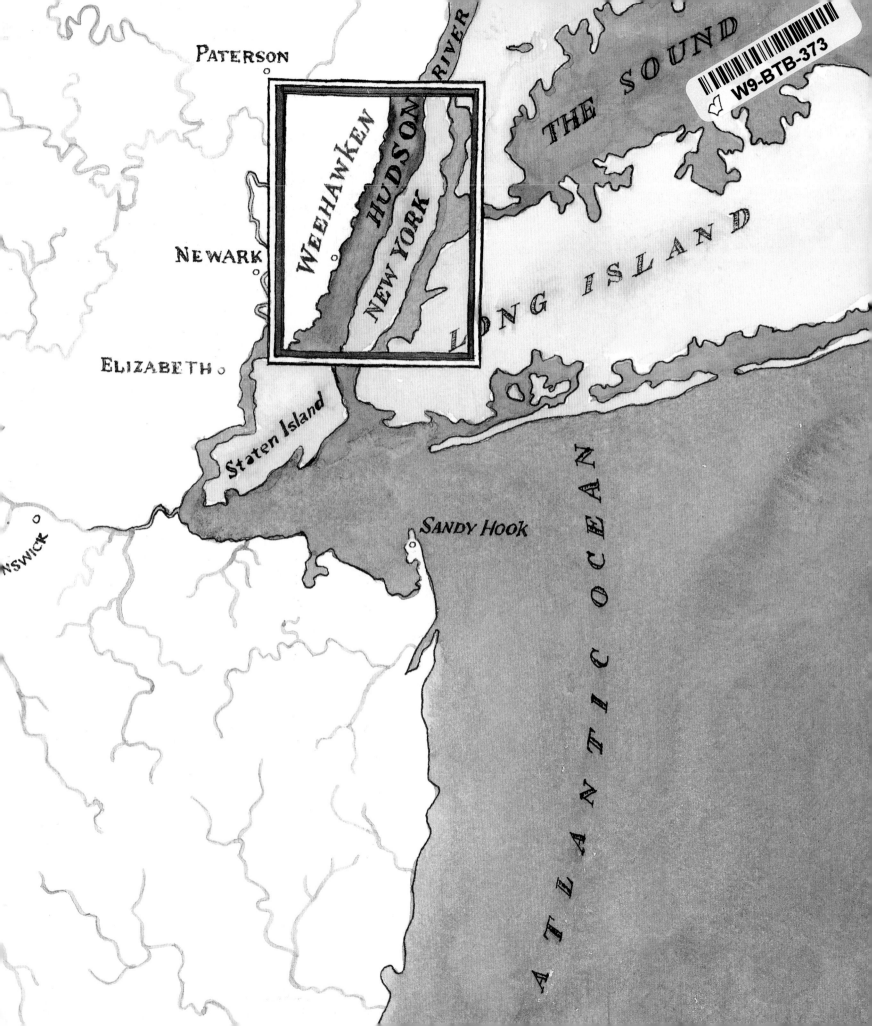

DUEL!

Burr and Hamilton's Deadly War of Words

DENNIS BRINDELL FRADIN

Illustrated by LARRY DAY

WALKER & COMPANY
New York

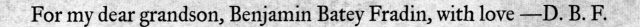

For my dear grandson, Benjamin Batey Fradin, with love —D. B. F.

For Eric Rohman —L. D.

First published in the United States of America in 2008 by Walker Publishing Company, Inc.
Distributed to the trade by Macmillan

For information about permission to reproduce selections from this book, write to
Permissions, Walker & Company, 175 Fifth Avenue, New York, New York 10010

Library of Congress Cataloging-in-Publication Data
Fradin, Dennis B.
Duel! : Burr and Hamilton's deadly war of words / by Dennis Brindell Fradin ;
illustrations by Larry Day.
p.   cm.
Audience: Grades 4–6.
ISBN-13: 978-0-8027-9583-0 • ISBN-10: 0-8027-9583-8 [hardcover]
ISBN-13: 978-0-8027-9584-7 • ISBN-10: 0-8027-9584-6 [reinforced]
1. Burr-Hamilton Duel, Weehawken, N.J., 1804—Juvenile literature. 2. Burr, Aaron,
1756–1836—Juvenile literature. 3. Hamilton, Alexander, 1757–1804—Juvenile literature.
I. Day, Larry, ill. II. Title.
E302.6.H2F73 2008   973.4´6092—dc22   2007037994

Book design by Nicole Gastonguay
Typeset in Historical
Art created using ink with watercolor and gouache

Visit Walker & Company's Web site at www.walkeryoungreaders.com

Printed in China
2 4 6 8 10 9 7 5 3 1 [hardcover]
2 4 6 8 10 9 7 5 3 1 [reinforced]

All papers used by Walker & Company are natural, recyclable products
made from wood grown in well-managed forests. The manufacturing processes
conform to the environmental regulations of the country of origin.

As the sun rises on a July morning in 1804, two men stand ten paces apart on a New Jersey cliffside. One is Alexander Hamilton, a signer of the Constitution. The other is Aaron Burr, the vice president of the United States. They are risking arrest— and their lives—to fight an illegal pistol duel.

The two enemies had much in common, starting with difficult childhoods. Hamilton was born on Nevis, a Caribbean island, in 1755. By the time Alexander was thirteen, his father had left and his mother had died. The lonely boy dreamed of sailing to America. When Alexander was seventeen, friends and relatives raised money for him to make the journey. After a nearly two-thousand-mile voyage, Alexander entered an academy in Elizabeth, New Jersey.

Burr was an orphan by the age of two. Born in Newark, New Jersey, in 1756, he was raised in Elizabeth by an uncle who whipped him for pelting neighbors with cherries and pulling other pranks. Aaron kept running away, but his uncle always tracked him down.

Aaron graduated from New Jersey's Princeton College just as Hamilton came to Elizabeth, in 1772.

After the American Revolution began in 1775, Burr and Hamilton both fought heroically for independence.

Burr took part in an attack on the British in Quebec, Canada. He was one of only two men in his unit's front ranks to survive British cannon fire.

At the Battle of Monmouth in New Jersey, Hamilton was badly injured when his horse was shot, pinning him to the ground. His bravery in combat won him the nickname "the Little Lion."

During the war, both men served as aides to General George Washington. Because he was foreign born, Hamilton felt that other leaders saw him as an outsider. He had a chip on his shoulder and quarreled with many people, including Washington. Even so, Washington was very fond of Hamilton and named him his chief aide. Burr was envious that Washington favored Hamilton. Washington thought Burr was a troublemaker and soon dismissed him from his staff.

After the war, the tension continued to build between Burr and Hamilton. Outwardly friendly, they battled each other as lawyers in New York City's courtrooms. Then their rivalry moved to the halls of government.

In 1787 Hamilton helped create the U.S. Constitution. Two years later President Washington named him first secretary of the treasury.

In 1791 Burr won a U.S. Senate seat, defeating Hamilton's father-in-law, Philip Schuyler. Convinced that Burr had run against his wife's father just to spite him, Hamilton was enraged. He wrote letters to lawmakers, calling Burr "the worst sort" of public figure.

Next, Burr ran for president in 1800. He and Thomas Jefferson tied for first place, and the U.S. House of Representatives had to choose the president.

Behind the scenes, Hamilton wrote notes calling Burr "wicked" and saying that "Mr. Burr loves nothing but himself." Worse yet, claimed Hamilton, Burr

would hurt the country if elected president. Partly due to Hamilton's attacks, Burr was defeated. Jefferson was elected president, and Burr had to settle for becoming vice president. When Burr found out about Hamilton's slurs against him, their secret fight became public.

Near the end of his vice presidency, Burr ran for governor of New York. Two of his friends caught Hamilton warning a group of lawmakers in Albany that, if elected, Burr would bring "rottenness" into New York politics. Soon after, a newspaper article reported that Hamilton had called Burr "despicable" at an Albany dinner party.

The next day, Burr lost the election for governor. He was furious that Hamilton's name-calling had again played a major role in his defeat.

Burr could have written a newspaper article blasting Hamilton or asked to meet with him to iron out their differences. Instead Burr sent Hamilton notes demanding that he apologize for his remarks—or fight a duel.

Hamilton could have apologized or arranged to meet with Burr to make peace. Instead he accepted Burr's challenge.

The date and place for the duel were set: Wednesday, July 11, 1804, in Weehawken, New Jersey, across the Hudson River from New York City.

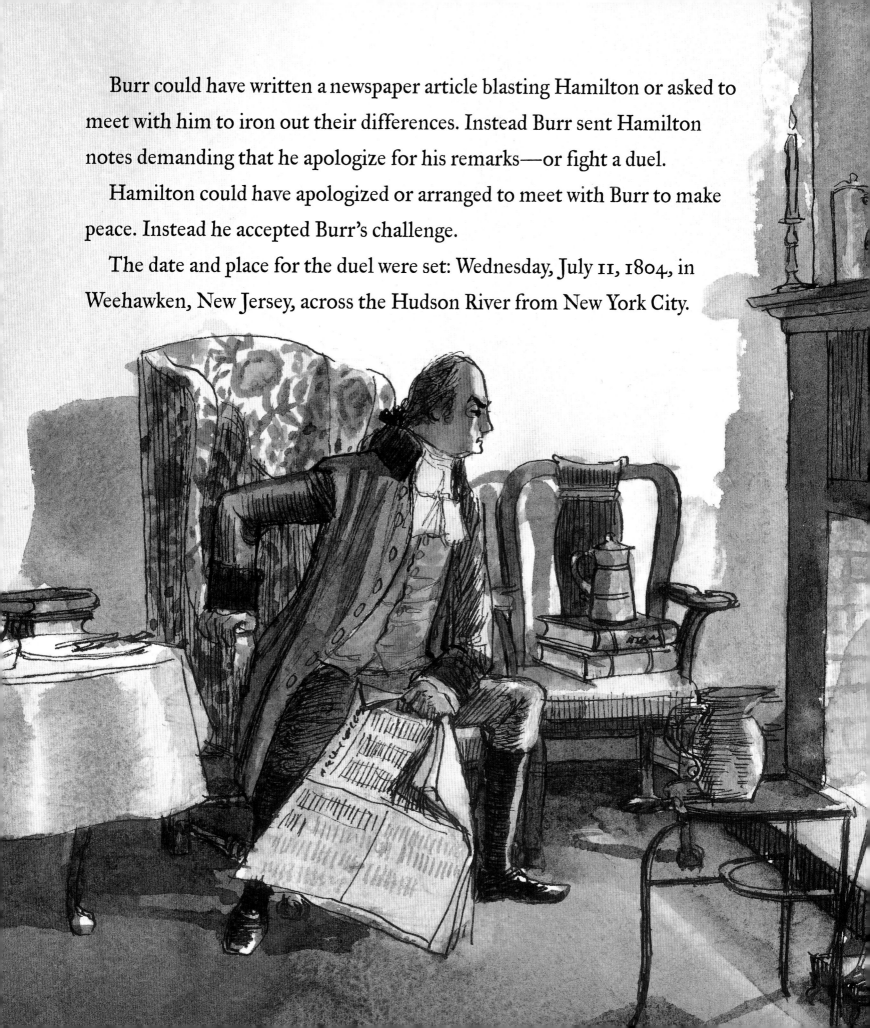

Knowing they might not survive the gunfight, Hamilton and Burr said farewell to their loved ones. Hamilton spent the Sunday before the duel with his family. On the eve of the duel, Burr wrote a parting letter to his daughter Theo.

Early the next morning, oarsmen row Hamilton and Burr across the Hudson from New York City to Weehawken in separate boats.

Hamilton and Burr each brought a second, or assistant. Hamilton's second prepares to give the signal for the duel to start.

"Ready?" he asks the men.

Burr nods. But the sun's glare is bothering Hamilton. "I beg pardon for delaying," he says, putting on his spectacles. Now both men await the word to fire.

The second repeats, "Ready?"

"Yes!" answer Hamilton and Burr.

Then they hear, "Present!"—the signal that they can aim and fire.

Burr and Hamilton fire their pistols. As the gun smoke clears, they both
stagger. It appears that they have shot each other.

Hamilton falls face-first to the ground, severely wounded. Burr,

however, has only stumbled on a stone and quickly regains his footing.

He starts toward Hamilton, but his second hurries him to their boat.

By remaining on the scene, the vice president risks arrest.

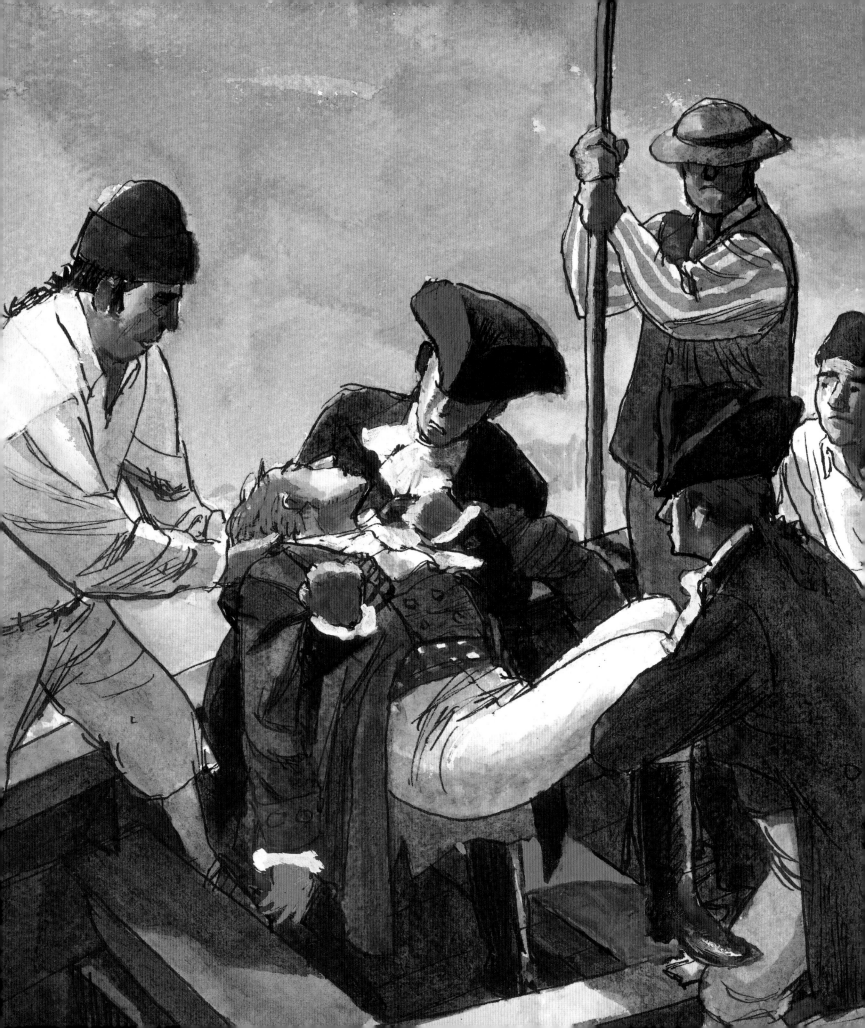

Hamilton's second carries him to their boat. He is rushed back to New York, where a doctor tends to him at a friend's house.

Hamilton calls for his wife and children, but when they arrive, he cannot speak. At two o'clock on the afternoon of July 12, 1804, he takes his last breath.

Burr was charged with issuing a challenge for a duel and with murder but was never brought to trial on either charge. Despite being illegal, dueling was tolerated by many people. Burr was even allowed to complete his term as vice president. However, the public's outrage over Hamilton's death destroyed any future in politics Burr might have had.

He then became involved in schemes to conquer territory within and beyond the United States, which led to his being charged with treason. Although he was found not guilty, his reputation was utterly ruined. Burr died a forgotten man in New York City at the age of eighty.

On the other hand, Hamilton's reputation soared after his death. Towns, streets, and parks were named for him. His portrait appears on ten-dollar bills. Today, few people realize that both men were at fault for the most famous duel in American history.

THE END OF DUELING

Dueling continued for about a century after Hamilton's death. In 1806 Andrew Jackson, later our seventh president, killed lawyer Charles Dickinson in a duel in Kentucky. Two Navy commodores, James Barron and Stephen Decatur, fought a duel in Maryland in 1820. Decatur, a war hero known for his comment, "Our country, right or wrong," was killed.

Abraham Lincoln *nearly* fought a sword duel with attorney James Shields on a Mississippi River island at the Illinois–Missouri border in 1842. Fortunately they had the sense to make up before anyone was hurt.

The Western gunfights in which two men faced off on a dusty street were a kind of duel of the late 1800s. Finally, by about 1900, dueling as a way to settle quarrels was, for the most part, abandoned.

BIBLIOGRAPHY

Burr, Samuel Engle, Jr. *The Burr-Hamilton Duel and Related Matters*. 2nd edition. San Antonio: The Naylor Company, 1971.

Fleming, Thomas. *Duel: Alexander Hamilton, Aaron Burr and the Future of America*. New York: Basic Books, 1999.

Hecht, Marie B. *Odd Destiny: The Life of Alexander Hamilton*. New York: Macmillan, 1982.

Randall, Willard Sterne. *Alexander Hamilton: A Life*. New York: HarperCollins, 2003.

Rogow, Arnold A. *A Fatal Friendship: Alexander Hamilton and Aaron Burr*. New York: Hill and Wang, 1999.

Syrett, Harold C., and Jean G. Cooke, editors. *Interview in Weehawken: The Burr-Hamilton Duel as Told in the Original Documents*. Middletown, CT: Wesleyan University Press, 1960.

Wandell, Samuel H., and Meade Minnigerode. *Aaron Burr* (2 volumes). New York: G. P. Putnam's Sons, 1925.

FOR FURTHER READING

Haugen, Brenda. *Alexander Hamilton*. Minneapolis: Compass Point Books, 2005.

Ingram, W. Scott. *Aaron Burr and the Young Nation*. San Diego: Blackbirch Press, 2002.

Jones, Veda Boyd. *Alexander Hamilton: First U.S. Secretary of the Treasury*. Philadelphia: Chelsea House, 2000.

Kallen, Stuart A. *Alexander Hamilton*. Edina, MN: ABDO & Daughters Publishing, 2000.

Melton, Buckner F., Jr. *Aaron Burr: The Rise and Fall of an American Politician*. New York: PowerKids Press, 2004.

Rosenberg, Pam. *Alexander Hamilton: Soldier and Statesman*. Chanhassen, MN: Child's World, 2004.